Tucholsky Wagner Zola Scott Sydow Freud Schlegel
Turgenev Fonatne Wallace Twain Walther von der Vogelweide Fouqué Friedrich II. von Preußen
Weber Freiligrath
Kant Ernst Frey
Fechner Fichte Weiße Rose von Fallersleben Richthofen Frommel
Hölderlin
Engels Fielding Eichendorff Tacitus Dumas
Fehrs Faber Flaubert
Eliasberg Ebner Eschenbach
Feuerbach Maximilian I. von Habsburg Fock Eliot Zweig Vergil
Ewald
Goethe Elisabeth von Österreich London
Mendelssohn Balzac Shakespeare Dostojewski Ganghofer
Lichtenberg Rathenau Doyle Gjellerup
Trackl Stevenson Hambruch
Mommsen Tolstoi Lenz Droste-Hülshoff
Thoma Hanrieder
von Arnim Hägele Hauff Humboldt
Dach Verne
Reuter Rousseau Hagen Hauptmann Gautier
Karrillon Garschin Defoe Baudelaire
Damaschke Descartes Hebbel
Hegel Kussmaul Herder
Wolfram von Eschenbach Dickens Schopenhauer Rilke George
Darwin Melville Grimm Jerome
Bronner Bebel Proust
Campe Horváth Aristoteles Voltaire Federer Herodot
Bismarck Vigny Barlach Heine
Gengenbach
Storm Casanova Tersteegen Gilm Grillparzer Georgy
Lessing Langbein Gryphius
Chamberlain Lafontaine
Brentano Claudius Schiller Kralik Iffland Sokrates
Strachwitz Schilling
Katharina II. von Rußland Bellamy Raabe Gibbon Tschechow
Gerstäcker
Löns Hesse Hoffmann Gogol Wilde Vulpius
Luther Heym Hofmannsthal Morgenstern Gleim
Roth Klee Hölty Goedicke
Luxemburg Heyse Klopstock Kleist
Machiavelli Puschkin Homer Mörike Musil
La Roche Horaz
Navarra Aurel Musset Kierkegaard Kraft Kraus
Lamprecht Kind Hugo Moltke
Nestroy Marie de France Kirchhoff
Laotse Ipsen Liebknecht
Nietzsche Nansen Ringelnatz
Marx Lassalle Gorki Klett
von Ossietzky May Leibniz
vom Stein Lawrence Irving
Petalozzi Knigge
Platon Kafka
Sachs Pückler Michelangelo Kock
Poe Liebermann Korolenko
de Sade Praetorius Mistral Zetkin

The publishing house tredition has created the series **TREDITION CLASSICS**. It contains classical literature works from over two thousand years. Most of these titles have been out of print and off the bookstore shelves for decades.

The book series is intended to preserve the cultural legacy and to promote the timeless works of classical literature. As a reader of a **TREDITION CLASSICS** book, the reader supports the mission to save many of the amazing works of world literature from oblivion.

The symbol of **TREDITION CLASSICS** is Johannes Gutenberg (1400 – 1468), the inventor of movable type printing.

With the series, tredition intends to make thousands of international literature classics available in printed format again – worldwide.

All books are available at book retailers worldwide in paperback and in hardcover. For more information please visit: www.tredition.com

tredition was established in 2006 by Sandra Latusseck and Soenke Schulz. Based in Hamburg, Germany, tredition offers publishing solutions to authors and publishing houses, combined with worldwide distribution of printed and digital book content. tredition is uniquely positioned to enable authors and publishing houses to create books on their own terms and without conventional manufacturing risks.

For more information please visit: www.tredition.com

Capitals A Primer of Information about Capitalization with some Practical Typographic Hints as to the Use of Capitals

Frederick W. (Frederick William) Hamilton

Imprint

This book is part of the TREDITION CLASSICS series.

Author: Frederick W. (Frederick William) Hamilton
Cover design: toepferschumann, Berlin (Germany)

Publisher: tredition GmbH, Hamburg (Germany)
ISBN: 978-3-8491-8411-7

www.tredition.com
www.tredition.de

CONTENTS

CAPITALS

INTRODUCTION

A capital letter is a letter of formal shape. Capitals were originally derived from the stiff and angular letters used in formal inscriptions. Originally all writing was done in capitals. Later the scribes devised less formal shapes for the letters, making use of lines more easily made by brush or pen on papyrus, parchment, or paper. The capitals were retained for certain uses but the less formal shapes were employed to do the greater part of the work. These less formal letters have been known by several names. They will be referred to here by that under which they are known to modern printers, "lower-case."

A further modification of the letter came with the introduction of the sloping, or italic letter. This received its name from its place of origin, Italy. It was introduced by Nicholas Jenson, a printer of Venice, and was an imitation of the handwriting of the Italian poet Petrarch. Originally it was used only for the lower-case and was combined with the older form of capital letters, called roman, also from the place of its origin. Later the italic characteristics were given to capitals as well as lower-case letters.

An ordinary font of book type contains five series of letters: full capitals, small capitals, italic capitals (full size), roman lower-case, and italic lower-case. The full capital, roman or italic, is larger than the other letters of the font, every letter being as high as the lower-case ascenders. The small capital is only as high as the lower-case round letters. Larger capitals still are sometimes used as chapter initials and the like.

It will be observed that the distinction between capital and lower-case letters is one of form, not of size. The full capitals being much more used than the small capitals and being larger than the other letters in the font, the impression [2] is common that the size is the distinguishing mark. This erroneous impression has even crept into dictionary definitions.

The full capital, which will hereafter be called in this book simply the capital, is used in combination with lower-case letters or with small capitals in the same word. The small capital is not used in combination with lower-case in the same word. We may print GEORGE WASHINGTON, George Washington, GEORGE WASH-INGTON, or George Washington, but not george washington.

In manuscript capitals are indicated by three lines under a word or letter, ▦and small capitals by two lines ▬. A single line ▬indicates that italics are to be used.

Originally the writers of manuscripts used capitals for ornament and variety in the text. They followed no rules but each writer was guided by his own judgment and sense of beauty. As the use of capitals gradually became systematized and reduced to rules, different systems were adopted in different countries. The use of capitals varies greatly in different languages. Attention will be mainly confined in this book to the usages followed in the printing of English. Attempts to point out the various differences to be found in German, French, etc. would only confuse the young apprentice.

These rules grow out of a fundamental principle.

The purpose of capitals is to emphasize the words in which they are employed. With the exception of the cases of the words *I* and *O*, which are capitalized for typographical reasons, this idea of calling special attention to a word, or words, for one reason or another will be found to be at the bottom of the variations in usage in different printing offices and by different writers. The same tendency is observable here which is so evident in style and in punctuation. Direct statements, simple sentences as free from involution and complication as possible, are more and more taking the place of the involved, complicated, and obscure sentences of old times. The ideal style of to-day consists of simple words simply arranged. Such a style needs little [3] pointing. The reader is quite able to find his way through the paragraph without constant direction. Punctuation marks are directions at the crossroads of thought. Consequently the punctuation mark is now much more sparingly used than formerly.

Just as we have found out that well chosen words can tell their story with very few marks of interpretation so we have found out that they can tell their story with very few marks of emphasis. The use of capitals has decreased greatly during the last two centuries and is constantly decreasing, and this tendency is likely to go still further. The great DeVinne whose books on *The Practice of Typography*, written ten to fifteen years ago, are still of the highest authority was thoroughly up-to-date in his methods and was remarkable for the restrained and refined good taste which characterized all his recommendations, but in some points restraint in the use of capitals has gone even beyond his precepts.

It is worth while to remember that the real implement of English speech is the word, not the point nor the letter form. Just to the extent that we rely on marks of punctuation and emphasis to convey our meaning we betray our ignorance of the really significant elements of the language. The schoolgirl says she "had a *perfectly splendid* time" at the dance, when she tells about it in her letter to her dearest friend. If "perfectly splendid" were a proper term to use in such a connection, which it is not, the words themselves would carry all the emphasis possible. Nothing could really be added to them by any typographical device. In the same way the common use of profanity among ignorant people probably arises mainly from a feeling that the ordinary words with which they are familiar are colorless and do not express their thoughts with sufficient emphasis

Just as emphasis in style is difficult when one habitually uses the strongest words and emphasis in voice is difficult when one habitually shouts, so emphasis in print is difficult when one habitually uses large capitals, display type, and italics. Loud printing is as objectionable as loud talking.

[4]

USE OF FULL CAPITALS

General uses:

1. Use a capital letter to begin every sentence and every word or group of words punctuated as a sentence.

Welcome! We are glad to see you.

This rule does not apply to literal reproductions of matter not originally conforming to it.

2. Use a capital letter to begin every line of poetry.

The Lord hates a quitter,
But he doesn't hate him, son,
When the quitter's quitting something
He shouldn't have begun.   [that

This rule does not apply to turned over lines like the third line in the stanza just preceding.

3. Use a capital letter to begin every quotation consisting of a complete sentence.

Ben Franklin says, "Honesty is the best policy."

The campaign was "a punitive expedition for the suppression of brigandage."

Capitalize:

1. Names of the Deity, of the members of the Trinity, of the Virgin Mary, and of the Devil, when a personal devil is referred to.

When the word devil is used as a general term or as an expletive the capital is not used.

2. Nouns and adjectives used to designate the Deity or any member of the Trinity:

the Almighty, the Ruler of the Universe, the Supreme Architect of the Universe, the Creator, Providence (personified), Heaven (personified, e. g., Heaven forbid!), Father, Son, Holy Ghost, Spirit, Messiah, and the like.

[5] The following list of words of this sort to be capitalized, taken from Mr. William Dana Orcutt's *The Writer's Desk Book* (Frederick A. Stokes, New York) will be found useful:

Almighty
Authorized Version
Common Version
Creator
Deity
Father
God

Holy Bible
Holy Spirit
Holy Writ
Jehovah
Jesus Christ
King
Logos
Lord
Messiah
Passover
Pentecost
Redeemer
Revised Version
Sabbath
Saviour
Scriptures
Son of Man
Son
Spirit
The Trinity
The Virgin Mary
Word

Care needs to be taken with words of this class. Particular attention should be paid to the wording of rule 2, just given. The same words in other senses or other connections are not capitalized. *Heaven* and *hell* and derived adjectives are not capitalized in their ordinary uses:

Adjectives and other derivatives from these words are not capitalized. We write *Messiah*, but *messianic* and *messiahship*; *Christology* but *christological*, *fatherhood*, *sonship*, and the like.

Such words as *deity*, *god*, and the like are not capitalized where any but the God of the Bible is referred to.

3. Pronouns referring to God, Christ, or the Holy Spirit in direct address or where there might otherwise be ambiguity.

These pronouns are not capitalized in the Bible. They are generally capitalized in hymn books and books of devotion. These pronouns were formerly all capitalized as a mark of respect to God whenever there was any mention of him, even indirect. The tendency is more and more to eliminate them except in the second person (direct address). In view of the change now going on it is best to follow copy if the author appears to have decided preferences.

[6] 4. Books, divisions, and versions of the Bible.

Book of Job, Twenty-third Psalm,
New Testament, Revised Version.

5. General biblical terms and titles of parables.

The Law, The Prophets, Major and Minor Prophets (referring to the collections of prophetic books), *Lord's Prayer, Lord's Supper, Parable of the Prodigal Son, the Beatitudes, the Priestly Code* and many other such terms.

Use lower-case for *biblical* and *scriptural.*

6. Capitalize *Holy* in *Holy place* and *Holy of holies.*

Say *Gospel of John,* but speak of the *gospel message.*

7. The names of religious bodies and their followers.

Catholic, Protestant, Unitarian, Methodist, Buddhists, Taoists, Lamas.

8. The names of monastic orders and their followers.

Jesuits, Brothers of the Common Life, Recollets, Crutched Friars, Cowley Fathers.

9. The word Church when it stands for the Church universal or is a part of the name of some particular denomination or organization.

For salvation he sought the Church.
The Church of Rome.
The First Presbyterian Church.
I was on my way to church.
He is a student of church history. (Note use of lower-case in this sentence.)

10. The names of creeds and professions of faith.

Apostle's Creed, Thirty-nine Articles, Nicene Creed.

Note that the adjective ante-Nicene is printed as it here appears.

11. The word "father" when used in direct reference to the fathers of the church, and to the Pilgrim leaders of New England, and the word "reformers" when used of the leaders of the Reformation.

The ante-Nicene Fathers.
Luther, Calvin and the other Reformers.

[7] The word "father" is not capitalized when the reference is general, as in the first sentence of this section.

The capitalization of "reformer" is intended to distinguish persons connected with a certain definite historical movement from persons interested in reform. Many persons might consider that the Reformers were not reformers.

12. Names of persons.

John Smith,
George V.

But write *John o' Groat, Tam o' Shanter,* and the like where *o'* is an abbreviation of *of* and not the Gælic *O'* as *O'Neil,* etc.

In writing foreign names which contain particles, capitalize the particles when not preceded by a Christian name or title.

Alfred de Musset but *De Musset,*
le Duc de Morny but *De Morny,*
Prince von Bismarck but *Von Bismarck.*

By exception the Dutch particle "van" is always capitalized.

Van Hoorn, Stephen Van Rensselær.

13. Epithets appended to proper names or substituted for them.

Frederick the Great
Peter the Hermit
William Red Head (Rufus)
the Conqueror.

14. Names of races of men.

Aryan, Caucasian, etc., but generally *negro* and *gypsy*, by exception.

15. Names of places.

a. Cities, rivers, oceans, lakes, mountains, etc.

Chicago
Mississippi River
Atlantic Ocean
Lake Superior
Pike's Peak
Strawberry Hill.

[8] Note that the generic terms ocean, lake, mountain and the like are capitalized only when they are an actual part of the name itself. We would say *"The Atlantic Ocean lies east of the United States,"* but we would say *"The states which form the North American republic look out on two great oceans, the Atlantic and the Pacific."*

The following tables are taken from *A Manual for Writers* by John Matthews Manley and John Arthur Powell (University of Chicago Press, Chicago).

Subject to the rule just stated, they will be found very useful.

Capitalize, in singular form only, when immediately following the name

Archipelago
Borough
Branch (stream)
Butte
Canyon
County
Crater
Creek
Delta
Forest
Fork
Gap
Glacier

Gulch
Harbor
Head
Hollow
Mesa
Narrows
Ocean
Parish (La.)
Park
Plateau
Range
Reservation
Ridge
River
Run

Capitalize in singular or plural form when immediately following the name

Hill
Island
Mountain
Spring

Capitalize, in singular form, either before or after the name; and in plural form before the name

Bay
Bayou
Camp (military)
Cape
Dalles
Desert
Falls
Fort
Isle
Lake
Mount
Oasis

Pass
Peak
Point
Port
Sea
Strait
Valley
Volcano

b. Names of streets, squares, parks, buildings, etc.

Amsterdam Avenue
Van Buren Street
Independence Square
Lincoln Park
Transportation Building.

[9] The same rule as to capitalization of the generic name holds here as in the preceding section. The usual tendency to drop capitals is at work here and newspapers now write *Washington street* and *Federal building*. It is very probable that the capitals will finally be dropped from the generic terms wherever used.

Printers should keep a careful watch on the usage of the best offices so as to keep advised as to the progress of these changes.

c. Nouns, and adjectives derived from them designating recognized geographical divisions of a country or of the world.

East, West, North, South,
Westerner, Oriental.

When these words are used in their ordinary significance of mere direction or location they are not capitalized except that in writing of Biblical history we speak of the *Northern Kingdom* and the *Southern Kingdom* into which Solomon's territory was split after his death.

16. Generic terms for political divisions.

a. When the term is part of the name and directly follows it.

Holy Roman Empire
British Empire
Northwest Territory
Queen's County.

b. When it is used with the preposition of in such phrases as *Borough of the Bronx, Department of the Gulf.*

c. When part of a nickname, *The Crescent City, the Buckeye State, the City of Brotherly Love.*

Be careful not to capitalize such words when they are not an actual part of the name. *French Republic* is the name of the county, exactly translating *Republique Francaise,* but *American republic* is not such a name. You would write *State of New York* in a legal document in which the state would be considered as a corporate person, but in ordinary references it would be *state of New York.*

[10] 17. The days of the week and the months of the year, but not the seasons unless personified.

Monday the fifth of August.
April is the first month of spring.
Spring, beautiful Spring.

But write *ten o'clock, nine a.m., ten p.m.*

18. Festivals and historic or famous days.

Easter Day
Fast Day
Independence Day
Black Friday.

19. Stars, planets, constellations, and the like, except *sun, moon, stars, earth.*

Mars, the Milky Way, the Pleiades.

20. Ordinal numbers used to designate numbered political divisions, sessions of Congress, names of regiments, Egyptian dynasties, and the like.

Second Congressional District,
First Ward, Ninth Precinct, Forty-third
Congress, Sixth Massachusetts Regiment,
Fifth Dynasty.

21. Names of genera but not of species: except that in botanical and zoölogical copy the species may be capitalized if derived from a proper name.

Agaricus campestris
Parkinsonia Torreyana
Pterygomatopus schmidti, (Medical).

The English derivatives from these scientific words are not capitalized. We write of the *agarics,* the *felids,* the *carnivores,* etc.

22. *Father, mother,* and other words denoting relationship when used with a proper name or without a personal pronoun.

I saw Aunt Lucy and Cousin Charles.
I saw my aunt Lucy and my cousin Charles.
I have received a letter from my mother.
I have received a letter from Mother.

[11] 23. Names of political parties and of philosophical, literary, and artistic schools, and their adherents.

Republican, National Liberal, Social Democrats, Stoics (but *neo-Platonism, pseudo-Christianity,* etc.) *the Lake school, the Romantic movement, the Symbolic school of painters.*

24. Political and historical designations which have been much used and have come to have special significances such as names of leagues, parties, classes, movements, and the like.

Holy Alliance, Dreibund, Roundheads, Independents, Reformation, Dissenter.

25. Names of well-known historic epochs, periods in the history of language, and geological ages and strata. The word "age" is not capitalized except when necessary to avoid ambiguity.

Stone age, Middle Ages, Age of Elizabeth, Crusades, Commune (of Paris), Middle English, Neolithic.

26. Names of important events.

Hundred Years War, Battle of Trenton,
Louisiana Purchase, Norman Conquest.

27. Names of specific treaties, important laws, and the like.

Peace of Amiens, Edict of Nantes, Concordat, Emancipation Proclamation, Fourteenth Amendment.

28. Names of governmental bodies and departments and their branches when specifically designated.

Congress, the Senate, the Board of Aldermen, the House of Commons, the Committee on Education.

Care must be taken to distinguish between these specific references and general uses of the same word.

The state legislature of Massachusetts is officially termed the General Court.

The matter was referred to the War Department but was sent back on the ground that it belonged to another department.

[12] 29. The official titles of corporations, organizations, and institutions, social, religious, educational, political, business, and the like.

Knights Templars, Knights of Columbus, Associated Charities, Cook County Normal School, Society for the Prevention of Cruelty to Animals, Chicago, Rock Island and Pacific Railroad.

In long titles, like the last example given, the important words are capitalized as in book titles (see Sec. 31). Use capitals when referring to such organizations by initials, *C. R. I. & P. R. R.* Here again it must be remembered that the capitals are used in specific references only.

The Young People's Society of Christian Endeavor of the Third Congregational Church.

The young people's societies connected with the Congregational church-es do great good.

30. The names of conventions, congresses, expositions, etc.

Parliament of Religions,
International Peace Congress,
Panama-Pacific Exposition.

31. The first words, principal words, and last word in English tides of books and other publications; of their divisions (parts, chapters, cantos, etc.); of the topics of speeches, sermons, toasts, and the like; of pictures; of plays; of musical compositions, etc.

In long titles nouns and pronouns are capitalized always; verbs, participles, and adverbs usually; articles, prepositions and conjunctions never.

Standard Thesaurus of English Words and Phrases, Science and Health with Key to the Scriptures, Lincoln's Gettysburg Address, Paradise Lost, Measure for Measure, A New Way to Pay Old Debts, The Coronation of Charles VII at Rheims, the Moonlight Sonata.

[13] The word "the" is capitalized when it forms an actual part of the title of a book but not otherwise.

The Printer's Dictionary. The Life and Times of Charles V. the Review of Reviews, the Laacoon, the Fifth Symphony.

32. Dedications; headings of parts and chapters; headings of many important minor parts of a book.

To All Who Love Good Printing.
Chapter Twenty-Seven.
Part Three.
The Invention of Movable Types.
The Practical Value of Gutenberg's Invention.
(These last as sections of a book on the origin
of printing).

33. In foreign languages the usage is somewhat different. The following rules will be found useful:

a. Always capitalize the first word.

b. In Latin capitalize only proper nouns and adjectives derived therefrom.

Commentarii Cæsaris de bello Gallico.

c. In French, Italian, Spanish, Swedish, and Norwegian, capitalize proper names but not adjectives derived therefrom.

La vie de Ronsard; Histoire de la litterature francaise, Novelle e racconti popolari italiani, Antologia de poetas liricos castellanos.

d. In German capitalize all nouns and all adjectives derived from the names of persons but not those derived from other proper nouns.

Geschichte des deutsches Reich
Die Homerische Frage.

e. In Danish capitalize all nouns.

f. In Dutch capitalize all nouns and all adjectives derived from proper nouns.

34. Titles of ancient manuscripts.

Codex Alexandrinus.

[14] 35. In titles of books, etc. all nouns forming parts of hyphenated compounds should be capitalized.

36. In side heads capitalize the first word and proper nouns only.

37. Personal titles as follows:

a. Titles preceding a name and so forming part of it.

King George V.
Pope Benedict XV.
Duke William of Aquitaine.

But not otherwise.

Woodrow Wilson, president of the United States, the emperor of Germany, the present king of Spain is Alfonso XIII.

b. Titles used in place of the name with reference to a particular person or to the present holder of an office.

I hope when in Rome to see the Pope.
He hoped some day to become pope.

c. Familiar names applied to a particular person.

the Father of his Country.
Unser Fritz.
the Little Corporal.

d. Orders of knighthood and titles attached to them.

Knight of the Garter,
Knight Commander of St. Michael and St. George.

e. Titles used in direct address.

Good morning, Mr. President.

f. Academic degrees in abbreviated form following a name.

David Starr Jordan, Ph. D., LL. D.

So also letters following a name indicating membership of certain scientific and artistic organizations.

F. R. G. S. (Fellow of the Royal Geographic Society).
R. A. (Member of the Royal Academy).

So also in the United States and Great Britain, *M. C.* (Member of Congress) and *M. P.* (Member of Parliament).

. [15] Where a person has many titles the following of this rule involves certain difficulties. Such a name as

John Smith, A. M., D. D., Ph. D., L. H. D., D. C. L., LL. D. is by no means impossible.

In such a case the titles become much more prominent than the name and the page is disfigured by the spotty appearance of the text. Small capitals may sometimes be used with good effect in such a case but this should not be done without obtaining proper permission.

The difficulty of handling these long and numerous titles in the composition of title pages is sometimes considerable. Three methods of dealing with the difficulty are open.

a. The honorary titles may be put in capitals regardless of the unsightly appearance of the line.

b. The honorary titles may be put in a small size of the same face and justified in the line. This lessens the undue prominence of the titles, but puts the line out of balance.

c. The honorary titles may be put in a separate line, or lines, below the name, set in small type, and spelled out in full. It is not necessary to capitalize *jr.* and *sr.* in lower-case text matter unless so desired by the author.

In compound titles capitalize each word if it would be capitalized separately.

Major General Leonard Wood,
Chief Justice Taney,
Commander-in-Chief Field
Marshal Sir John French.

38. Names of things personified.

Nature, Vice, Thrift, and the like.

39. Adjectives derived from proper nouns.

The Elizabethan age.
Roman law.

[16] Such adjectives and even proper nouns themselves lose the capital when they are applied as trade or scientific names to articles of common use or reference.

roman type, india ink, chinese white, volt, watt, boycott, platonic, bohemian.

40. The first word of a direct quotation.

As he turned to go he said: "Farewell, we shall never meet again."

41. The first word after "Whereas" and "Resolved" in resolutions.

WHEREAS. It has pleased God....
therefore be it
RESOLVED, That....

42. The first word after a colon when the colon introduces a logically complete phrase not very closely connected with what precedes.

My conclusion is: A policy of consistent neutrality is the only proper one for the country.

As the proverb well says: Beware the anger of a patient man.

43. *O* interjection, but not *oh* unless it begins a sentence.

In Latin sentences of exclamation, denunciation or appeal the lower-case *o* is used.

O tempora, o mores temporum.

44. The first personal pronoun *I* wherever it occurs.

45. Emphasized words.

We stand for Liberty and Union.

This use should be avoided except for advertising display, or job work.

We call attention to our Stock of Boots, Shoes, and Furnishings.

[17]

SMALL CAPITALS

The use of small capitals presents its own peculiar problems to the printer. The small capital has the form of the large capital but without its size and conspicuousness. The small capitals are ordinarily no taller than the round letters of the lower-case. They are usually on a smaller set, with a lighter face and obscured by more connecting lines. In many fonts of type they are really the weakest and least distinguished of all the five series. Wide enough to cover the body of the type fairly thoroughly in most letters and thus to reduce the apparent space between letters, without ascenders and without descenders, they are very monotonous and singularly ineffective when used in any considerable quantity. When used in masses it is at times even difficult to read them.

The use of small capitals is quite different from that of large ones. For the reasons just given they are not suited to display. For this purpose they are no better than italics, if as good. Owing to their lack of striking appearance and commanding quality they are not used for emphasis. Display and emphasis it will be remembered are the two principal uses of the full capital.

Small capitals are used more for variety than for display. They are commonly used for:

Side heads

Running titles

Catch lines of title pages when particular display is not desired.

They are sometimes used for the first word after a blank line, especially for the first word of a new chapter.

Long quotations of poetry are often printed with the first word in small capitals. In this, as in the preceding case, [18] the whole word is printed in small capitals except the first letter which is a full capital.

Proper names standing at the beginning of a chapter, occasionally even of a paragraph, are sometimes spelled in capitals or small capitals. If small capitals are used the initials of the name are put in full capitals.

Until within a comparatively short time tables of contents were often set in small capitals. At the same time it was customary to give a fairly full synopsis of the contents of each chapter under the chapter head. The result was a very monotonous page, dull, dense, hard to read. It is much better and now more common to use small caps for the chapter heads and ordinary text type for abstracts, using dashes or dots to separate the phrases in the synopsis and beginning each phrase with a capital.

The following reproduction of a part of a page from the table of contents of DeVinne's *Modern Methods of Book Composition* shows this method of treatment.

CONTENTS

[19] Where chapter synopses are not given, ordinary text type may be used for the table of contents.

The following reproduction of the table of contents of DeVinne's *Correct Composition* shows this method of treatment.

CONTENTS

[20] Small capitals are best for subheads when of not more than two lines. If the subheads are longer it is best to use lower-case.

Signatures and credits are often put in small capitals. It is usually, however, better to use italics for the purpose. There is no need of a dash to connect the name with the quotation. When two or more quotations from the same author are used as mottoes, with reference to the works from which they are taken or the occasion on which they were said, the name of the author may be put in small capitals in a separate line, the name of the book or speech in italics, and the occasion in smaller roman type.

Numerous signatures to a document or petition, such as the *Mayflower Compact* or the *Declaration of Independence*, are often set in columns using capitals for the initials and small capitals for the rest of the name. Full capitals are too large for the purpose.

We therefore, the Commissioners for the Massachusetts, Connecticut, and New Haven, do also, for our several governments, subscribe unto these.

John Winthrop, Governor of the Massachusetts
Thomas Dudley Theophilus Eaton
George Fenwick Edward Hopkins
Thomas Gregson

Dedications of books are commonly set in small capitals. As these dedicatory formulas are ordinarily brief there should be wide leading, good display, and care as to margins. The author will often give very definite specifications as to the arrangement of his copy in lines, and this will sometimes cause difficulty, occasionally compelling the use of too small type. The author's specifications must be followed if he adheres to them.

Small capitals are much favored for running titles of pages. Full capitals are much more effective and are to be preferred where the words are few. Small capitals of 12 or 14 point body are distinct but smaller sizes are crowded and hard to read. This difficulty can sometimes be remedied by hair spacing. Over spacing of such lines is objectionable though it has sometimes prevailed as a temporary fashion.

[21] Small capitals used in running titles are exposed to heavy wear and their shallow counters are liable to get choked up with ink. Capitals of the monotint or of a light-faced antique are sometimes selected for books frequently reprinted where the wear on the exposed running titles is very severe.

In reprinting letters it is common to use small capitals for the name of the place from which the letter was written, for the name of the addressee, and for the signature. In job and advertising work the name of the month and day and date are generally put in lower-case of the text letter. This rule is not followed, however, in books. When the heading of the letter is very long lower-case letters are preferable to small capitals under the general rules of taste which govern the use of types. The salutation, *Dear Sir, Gentlemen,* or the like, does not need small capitals. It is better printed in italic lower-case with a colon (not followed by a dash) at the end. If the matter is double leaded the salutation may go in a line by itself, otherwise conforming to the rules just given.

Reprints of formal inscriptions on tablets and the like are often made in small capitals surrounded by a border. There should be a good relief of white space between the type and the border.

In the Bible and in hymn books the words Lord and God are usually set with full capital initial and the rest of the word in small capitals.

This is, of course, a method of showing veneration and at one time it was customary to print all names of spiritual or temporal dignitaries and magnates or even ordinary names in small capitals. This practice still lingers in a few newspapers which print the names of persons, even those of small consequence, in small capitals, especially on the editorial page.

The tendency is steady toward the discriminating use of capitals, small capitals, and italics. More and more we restrict the use of marks of emphasis to the really necessary places leaving the words to tell their story without outside aid.

[22]

SUGGESTIONS AS TO TYPOGRAPHIC USE OF CAPITALS

Capitals are too strong to be used with Arabic numerals. This fault of proportion is increased by the custom of casting Arabic numerals on an en body for table work, making them only half as thick as the type. Full capitals may be used with full figures the width of an ordinary letter. Condensed capitals may be used with en body numerals.

If old-style capitals and figures are required in the same line use figures about one-half larger in body than the capitals and justify them to the line.

It is this difficulty in combining capitals and Arabic numerals in the same line that causes the extensive use of Roman numerals in chapter numbers, numbers of other headings, dates on title pages, and the like.

When a large initial three or four lines high is used for the first letter of a new chapter, large capitals are sometimes used, although such usage is not free from the reproach of looking too much like newspaper advertising. When this initial is a two line letter it should be in alignment with the small capitals of the upper line and the base line of the text letter of the lower line.

AMONG the earliest methods of communicating ideas to the absent pictures hold the largest place.

THERE comes a tide in the affairs of men which, taken at the flood, leads on to fortune.

Care should be taken not to compact capitals. Use wider leading and broader spacing than for lower-case; for example, where you would use one lead between lower-case lines you should use two or three between lines of capitals.

[23] Capitals occupy more of the type-body than lower-case letters and consequently words or lines set entirely with capitals need wider spacing and leading than the lower-case to make composition readable. When lines of roman capitals are set solid or single-leaded the en-quad will usually be enough space between words especially if the words are short; but for wide-leaded lines and head-lines double spaces (two three-to-em) will be needed. A head-line of round, open capitals may even need em-quad spaces. Wide letter words require wide spaces and words of thin or condensed letters require thin spaces.

UNITED TYPOTHETAE OF AMERICA

UNITED TYPOTHETAE OF AMERICA

Words which begin or end with A Y L V W T may need spaces a little less than those with H I M, etc. In small types the inequalities in white space beside or between combinations like L Y A T W and letters with regular shape like H I M N, may not be readily noticed, but in large sizes of capitals these differences are greatly increased and will often make unequal white spaces in a line with uniform metal spaces. In some styles of types a line may need unequal metal spaces in order to space the words evenly.

(Marks indicate insertion of spaces.)

TEN MAIL TRAINS

This line has en-quads between the words, but the forms
of L and T make the white space greater than
between the first and second words.

TEN MAIL TRAINS

This line has an en-quad in first space and three-to-em
in the second, with hair-spaces between some
letters of the words.

[24] So, also, it will often be necessary to insert pieces of paper, card, or thin leads between the letters of a word in large display, in order to make them evenly spaced, as shown in these examples:

(Marks indicate insertion of spaces.)

PLAINLY

PLAINLY

UNEVENLY SPACED

EVENLY SPACED

This differential spacing in a line of capitals will also be required in a line having abbreviations or initials. The following line, spaced with en-quads throughout, has unnecessarily wide spaces between the initials:

JOHN ENDICOTT LODGE, A. O. U. W.

Spaced with four-to-em in the last three places, it is improved:

JOHN ENDICOTT LODGE, A. O. U. W.

Capitals used as initials of titles and for other abbreviations, with the accompanying periods, should be thin-spaced or set close together, as shown in the second of these examples:

GEORGE MARKHAM, D. D., PH. D.

GEORGE MARKHAM, D. D., PH. D.

JOHN FLINT, M. D. V., BOSTON, U. S. A.

JOHN FLINT, M. D. V., BOSTON, U. S. A.

[25] Two or more lines of capitals of the same size should be spaced as nearly alike as possible. These three lines are so disproportionately spaced that they are not pleasing:

NORTH END UNION
B O S T O N
M A S S A C H U S E T T S

The squaring up is arbitrary and strained. The lines are better like
this:

NORTH END UNION
BOSTON
MASSACHUSETTS

But if it is necessary to square up lines and no additional words
or letters can be inserted the short line may be filled with florets or
other characters which should not be bolder than the type itself and
should be of a style to harmonize with it as nearly as possible.

NORTH END UNION
✾ ✾ ✾ BOSTON ✾ ✾ ✾
MASSACHUSETTS

The extra wide spacing of words set in capitals, as in head-lines
and running-heads, should be avoided by the young compositor;
there are places where it may be unobjectionable but it will require
good judgment and some experience to prevent such lines making
the page look freakish or amateurish.

[26] In jobbing, advertisement, and display work, capitals are used more freely than in plain reading matter. In book work the practice is to use capitals more freely than in newspaper composition. A study of the reading columns of daily newspapers will discover that capitals are used very sparingly and words are "kept down" in many cases which in more formal book and pamphlet work would be capitalized.

In advertisements, announcements, and circular letters, words are often capitalized for distinction or emphasis, as in these examples:

Those who win a Second or First Prize through a monthly or special contest become Honor Members of the Guild, and receive the Guild badge without charge.

You are cordially invited to attend the Spring Opening of Suits and Outside Garments for Women, on Wednesday and Thursday, April 28 and 29, in our new Mason Street Annex.

Precise rules for the use of capitals cannot be given for work of all kinds. Their insertion or omission will be governed greatly by the subject matter and the style of treatment desired by the proof-reader or the customer and the compositor's duty will not go further than to maintain some consistency in their use in each piece of work. When he has copy in which capitals are used as in the following example he will be expected either to discard all capitals except at the beginning of the sentences or to capitalize the words as in the second example:

Fifty styles of the Smartest and nobbiest wheel specialties for ponies and Small horses, Pony carts, light horse novelties, traps, wagons, Harness, Saddles, etc.

[27]

Fifty Styles of the Smartest and Nobbiest Wheel Specialties for Ponies and Small Horses, Pony Carts, Light Horse Novelties, Traps, Wagons, Harness, Saddles, etc.

In lines of large display, like head-lines, set in capitals and lower-case, all the important words should begin with capitals. Unimportant words, such as *of, the, by, for, but, in,* etc., except when they are at the beginning of the displayed phrase, are not capitalized.

Notice to the Public
The Best is the Cheapest
A Great Bargain in Hats
By Right of Conquest
For Love and Honor

A line of capitals containing an abbreviation or other short word should have capitals throughout when possible, as in the second form of these examples:

JOHN SMITH, Jr. JOHN SMITH, JR.
ROBINSON & Co. ROBINSON & CO.

In advertisement display lines like the following are permissible:

The GOLDEN HARVESTER
REGAL SHOES for Men

Combinations of different sizes and styles of types are also common and serve their purpose properly, as in this style, often used in billheads, etc.

to THOMAS W. ABBOTT, dr.
In account with FRANK ABBOTT

[28] Combinations of large and small capitals and lower-case like the following are, however, not approved:

william brown, President

The words in small capitals as well as the word in lower-case should begin with large capitals, like this:

William Brown, President

When lines of capitals are used in books and pamphlets, for headings and display, they should be used consistently—that is, all headings of a similar kind should be alike in any piece of work, and not one heading in capitals and another in lower-case. The composi tion of a title page is more pleasing when its chief lines are in one style of letters, giving a harmonious effect. When lines of capitals and lines of lower-case are interspersed in a page an appearance of confusion is liable to be the result.

[29]

SUPPLEMENTARY READING

A Manual for Writers. By John Matthews Manley and John Arthur Powell. The University of Chicago Press, Chicago.

The Writer's Desk Book. By William Dana Orcutt. Frederick Stokes Company, New York.

Correct Composition. By Theodore L. DeVinne. The Oswald Publishing Company, New York.

A Handbook of Composition. By Edwin D. Woolley. D. C. Heath, Boston.

Punctuation. With Chapters on Hyphenization, Capitalization and Spelling. By F. Horace Teale. Appleton & Co., New York.

[30]

QUESTIONS

As the subject matter of this book is such that many of the questions will serve only to bring out the accuracy of the pupil's memory of rules it is very desirable that care should be taken to insure intelligent use and application of the rules. To be able to repeat a rule is of very little importance compared with the ability to apply it intelligently.

The instructor should give the pupils constant practice in the application of these rules. This should consist of; —

> (a) Study of passages taken from all kinds of printed matter.

> (b) Rewriting of passages given out without capitalization.

In the first case a wide range of material should be used from the most carefully printed books to the most carelessly printed matter that can be found, including newspapers of varying excellence and pure advertising matter. The capitalization found should be studied and explained by the rules and the criticisms or changes suggested justified in the same way.

In like manner in the second case every capital used in the rewritten text should be justified by the proper rule.

Without such exercises as these, the book will have comparatively little value.

1. What is a capital letter?

2. How many series of letters does an ordinary font of type contain?

3. Name them, and tell what you know about each one.

4. In what does the distinction between capital and lower-case letter consist?

5. What combinations of capitals and lower-case are permissible?

6. In manuscript how do you indicate capitals? Italics?

7. What are capitals used for?

8. What tendencies are observable in style?

9. What is the real implement of English speech?

10. What are the general rules for the use of capitals?

11. Capitalize, *men pray to god, to christ and to the virgin mary that they may be defended by the holy ghost from those assaults of the devil which would make devils of them.* Give the rule for so doing.

[31] 12. Capitalize, *the supreme architect of the universe, sometimes called providence, has his own ways of bringing men to heaven.* Give the rule for so doing.

13. Learn the list of words under rule 2.

14. Are these words capitalized in all cases?

15. Are adjectives derived from these words capitalized?

16. When do you not capitalize *God* and its synonyms?

17. What is the usage as to pronouns referring to God and the other persons of the Trinity?

18. What is the rule regarding the Bible and matter related to it?

19. What is the rule regarding biblical terms?

20. Capitalize, *the holy man entered the holy place at the appointed time. The message of the gospel is found in the most spiritual form in the gospel of John.* Give the rule.

21. What is the rule about religious bodies and their members?

22. What is the rule about monastic orders?

23. What is the rule about *church*? Give examples of the different uses.

24. What is the rule about names of creeds?

25. Give different uses of *father* and *reformer* and explain them.

26. How do you use capitals in writing names of persons in English and in other languages?

27. What is the usage with regard to epithets and the like?

28. What is the usage with regard to races of men?

29. Give the rule for names of places, and examples of each usage.

30. Learn the tables under rule 15.

31. When do you capitalize generic terms for political divisions and when do you not?

32. What is the rule about words denoting time?

33. What is the rule about festivals, etc.?

34. What is the rule about astronomical terms?

35. When are ordinal numbers capitalized?

36. How are capitals used in scientific names?

37. What is the usage in such words as *father, mother,* and other terms denoting relationship?

[32] 38. What is the rule regarding names of parties, political, literary, etc.?

39. What is the rule as to historic parties, leagues, etc.?

40. What is the usage in writing of periods, historic, geological, etc.?

41. What is the usage regarding important events?

42. How are treaties, laws, etc., treated?

43. When are the names of governmental bodies, departments, etc., capitalized?

44. How are official titles of corporations and other bodies treated?

45. How are names of conventions, expositions, and the like treated?

46. How are capitals used in book titles and similar copy, including the use of *the*?

47. How are capitals used in dedications and headings?

48. Give the rules for the use of capitals in foreign book titles.

49. Give the rules for the use of capitals in personal titles.

50. What can you do when a name is followed by the initials of a number of titles?

51. What do you do in case of compound titles?

52. How do you write the names of things personified?

53. How are adjectives derived from proper nouns treated?

54. How are capitals used in direct quotations?

55. How are capitals used in resolutions?

56. Are capitals used after colons?

57. How do we write the interjections *O* and *oh*?

58. How do we write the first personal pronoun?

59. When and where are capitals used for emphasis?

60. Describe the peculiarities of small capitals.

61. Are they used in the same way as full capitals? Why?

62. What is the principal use of small capitals?

63. Give some of the places where small capitals are commonly used.

64. How are small capitals now used in tables of contents, and how were they formerly used?

[33] 65. What type would you use for a table of contents when chapter synopses are not given?

66. How are subheads treated?

67. How are signatures and credits treated?

68. How are dedications of books treated?

69. How are running titles treated?

70. What is good usage in reprinting letters?

71. What is a good way to set reprints of formal inscriptions?

72. What is the usage with regard to the names of persons treated with veneration?

73. What is the tendency in the use of capitals and other devices for emphasis?

74. How would you handle combinations of capitals and numerals, and why?

75. How would you treat large initials?

76. How should you space and lead capitals as compared with lower-case?

77. How should lines of capitals be spaced, and why?

78. Would capitals set with even spacing or without spacing appear to be evenly spaced?

79. What is the reason for the appearance just noted?

80. What would you do about it?

81. How should you space capitals used as initials of titles with accompanying periods?

82. How should you space two or more lines of capitals of the same size?

83. If squaring up is necessary, how should it be done?

84. What can you say about wide spacing of words set in capitals?

85. What can you say of the use of capitals in different sorts of matter?

86. How is the compositor guided in these cases?

87. How are capitals used in lines of large display?

88. How would you set a line of capitals containing an abbreviation or other short word?

89. How may capitals be used in lines of advertising display?

[34] 90. Under what circumstances are combinations of different sizes and styles of type permissible?

91. Are combinations of large and small capitals and lower-case advisable?

92. What rule should be followed when lines of capitals are used in books and pamphlets for headings and display?

[35]

GLOSSARY

Formal — Made in accordance with regular and established forms, or with dignity and impressiveness: stiff.

Genera — Plural of genus, a group for purposes of classification, embracing one or more species.

Generic — Of or pertaining to a genus (see genera) as distinct from specific, of or pertaining to a species (which see).

Ordinal — That form of the numeral that shows the order of anything in a series.

Species — A group for purposes of classification subordinate to a genus and composed of individuals having only minor differences.

Versions — (Of the Bible) Different translations of the original into the same or different languages.

[i]

TYPOGRAPHIC TECHNICAL SERIES
FOR APPRENTICES

The following list of publications, comprising the Typographic Technical Series for Apprentices, has been prepared under the supervision of the Committee on Education of the United Typothetae of America for use in trade classes, in course of printing instruction, and by individuals.

Each publication has been compiled by a competent author or group of authors, and carefully edited, the purpose being to provide the printers of the United States—employers, journeymen, and apprentices—with a comprehensive series of handy and inexpensive compendiums of reliable, up-to-date information upon the various branches and specialties of the printing craft, all arranged in orderly fashion for progressive study.

The publications of the series are of uniform size, 5×8 inches. Their general make-up, in typography, illustrations, etc., has been, as far as practicable, kept in harmony throughout. A brief synopsis of the particular contents and other chief features of each volume will be found under each title in the following list.

Each topic is treated in a concise manner, the aim being to embody in each publication as completely as possible all the rudimentary information and essential facts necessary to an understanding of the subject. Care has been taken to make all statements accurate and clear, with the purpose of bringing essential information within the understanding of beginners in the different fields of study. Wherever practicable, simple and well-defined drawings and illustrations have been used to assist in giving additional clearness to the text.

In order that the pamphlets may be of the greatest possible help for use in trade-school classes and for self-instruction, each title is accompanied by a list of Review Questions covering essential items of the subject matter. A short Glossary of technical terms belonging to the subject or department treated is also added to many of the books.

These are the Official Text-books of the United Typothetae of America.

Address all orders and inquiries to Committee on Education, United Typothetae of America, Chicago, Illinois, U. S. A.

[ii]

A primer of information regarding the history and mechanical construction of platen printing presses, from the original hand press to the modern job press, to which is added a chapter on automatic presses of small size. 51 pp.; illustrated; 49 review questions; glossary.

- **7. Cylinder Printing Presses By Herbert L. Baker**

Being a study of the mechanism and operation of the principal types of cylinder printing machines. 64 pp.; illustrated; 47 review questions; glossary.

- **8. Mechanical Feeders and Folders By William E. Spurrier**

The history and operation of modern feeding and folding machines; with hints on their care and adjustments. Illustrated; review questions; glossary.

- **9. Power for Machinery in Printing Houses By Carl F. Scott**

A treatise on the methods of applying power to printing presses and allied machinery with particular reference to electric drive. 53 pp.; illustrated; 69 review questions; glossary.

- **10. Paper Cutting Machines By Niel Gray, Jr.**

A primer of information about paper and card trimmers, hand-lever cutters, power cutters, and other automatic machines for cutting paper, 70 pp.; illustrated; 115 review questions; glossary.

- **11. Printers' Rollers By A. A. Stewart**

A primer of information about the composition, manufacture, and care of inking rollers. 46 pp.; illustrated; 61 review questions; glossary.

- **12. Printing Inks By Philip Ruxton**

Their composition, properties and manufacture (reprinted by permission from Circular No. 53, United States Bureau of Standards); together with some helpful suggestions about the everyday use of printing inks by Philip Ruxton. 80 pp.; 100 review questions; glossary.

[iii]

• 13. How Paper is Made By William Bond Wheelwright

A primer of information about the materials and processes of manufacturing paper for printing and writing. 68 pp.; illustrated; 62 review questions; glossary.

• 14. Relief Engravings By Joseph P. Donovan

Brief history and non-technical description of modern methods of engraving; woodcut, zinc plate, halftone; kind of copy for reproduction; things to remember when ordering engravings. Illustrated; review questions; glossary.

• 15. Electrotyping and Sterotyping By Harris B. Hatch and A. A. Stewart

A primer of information about the processes of electrotyping and stereotyping. 94 pp.; illustrated; 129 review questions; glossaries.

PART II—*Hand and Machine Composition*

• 16. Typesetting By A. A. Stewart

A handbook for beginners, giving information about justifying, spacing, correcting, and other matters relating to typesetting. Illustrated; review questions; glossary.

• 17. Printers' Proofs By A. A. Stewart

The methods by which they are made, marked, and corrected, with observations on proofreading. Illustrated; review questions; glossary.

- **18. First Steps in Job Composition By Camille DeVéze**

Suggestions for the apprentice compositor in setting his first jobs, especially about the important little things which go to make good display in typography. 63 pp.; examples; 55 review questions; glossary.

- **19. General Job Composition**

How the job compositor handles business stationery, programs and miscellaneous work. Illustrated; review questions; glossary.

- **20. Book Composition By J. W. Bothwell**

Chapters from DeVinne's "Modern Methods of Book Composition," revised and arranged for this series of text-books by J. W. Bothwell of The DeVinne Press, New York. Part I: Composition of pages. Part II: Imposition of pages. 229 pp.; illustrated; 525 review questions; glossary.

- **21. Tabular Composition By Robert Seaver**

A study of the elementary forms of table composition, with examples of more difficult composition. 36 pp.; examples; 45 review questions.

- **22. Applied Arithmetic By E. E. Sheldon**

Elementary arithmetic applied to problems of the printing trade, calculation of materials, paper weights and sizes, with standard tables and rules for computation, each subject amplified with examples and exercises. 159 pp.

- **23. Typecasting and Composing Machines A. W. Finlay, Editor**

Section I — The Linotype **By L. A. Hornstein**
Section II — The Monotype **By Joseph Hays**
Section III — The Intertype **By Henry W. Cozzens**

Section IV—Other Typecasting and Typesetting Machines
By Frank H. Smith

A brief history of typesetting machines, with descriptions of their mechanical principles and operations. Illustrated; review questions; glossary.

PART III—*Imposition and Stonework* [iv]

- ### 24. Locking Forms for the Job Press By Frank S. Henry

Things the apprentice should know about locking up small forms, and about general work on the stone. Illustrated; review questions; glossary.

- ### 25. Preparing Forms for the Cylinder Press By Frank S. Henry

Pamphlet and catalog imposition; margins; fold marks, etc. Methods of handling type forms and electrotype forms. Illustrated; review questions; glossary.

PART IV—*Presswork*

- ### 26. Making Ready on Platen Presses By T. G. McGrew

The essential parts of a press and their functions; distinctive features of commonly used machines. Preparing the tympan, regulating the impression, underlaying and overlaying, setting gauges, and other details explained. Illustrated; review questions; glossary.

- ### 27. Cylinder Presswork By T. G. McGrew

Preparing the press; adjustment of bed and cylinder, form rollers, ink fountain, grippers and delivery systems. Underlaying and overlaying; modern overlay methods. Illustrated; review questions; glossary.

- ### 28. Pressroom Hints and Helps By Charles L. Dunton

Describing some practical methods of pressroom work, with directions and useful information relating to a variety of printing-press problems. 87 pp.; 176 review questions.

• 29. Reproductive Processes of the Graphic Arts By A. W. Elson

A primer of information about the distinctive features of the relief, the intaglio, and the planographic processes of printing. 84 pp.; illustrated; 100 review questions; glossary.

PART V — *Pamphlet and Book Binding*

• 30. Pamphlet Binding By Bancroft L. Goodwin

A primer of information about the various operations employed in binding pamphlets and other work in the bindery. Illustrated; review questions; glossary.

• 31. Book Binding By John J. Pleger

Practical information about the usual operations in binding books; folding; gathering, collating, sewing, forwarding, finishing. Case making and cased-in books. Hand work and machine work. Job and blank-book binding. Illustrated; review questions; glossary.

PART VI — *Correct Literary Composition*

• 32. Word Study and English Grammar By F. W. Hamilton

A primer of information about words, their relations, and their uses. 68 pp.; 84 review questions; glossary.

• 33. Punctuation By F. W. Hamilton

A primer of information about the marks of punctuation and their use, both grammatically and typographically. 56 pp.; 59 review questions; glossary.

[v]

• 34. Capitals By F. W. Hamilton

A primer of information about capitalization, with some practical typographic hints as to the use of capitals. 48 pp.; 92 review questions; glossary.

- **35. Division of Words By F. W. Hamilton**

Rules for the division of words at the ends of lines, with remarks on spelling, syllabication and pronunciation. 42 pp.; 70 review questions.

- **36. Compound Words By F. W. Hamilton**

A study of the principles of compounding, the components of compounds, and the use of the hyphen. 34 pp.; 62 review questions.

- **37. Abbreviations and Signs By F. W. Hamilton**

A primer of information about abbreviations and signs, with classified lists of those in most common use. 58 pp.; 32 review questions.

- **38. The Uses of Italic By F. W. Hamilton**

A primer of information about the history and uses of italic letters. 31 pp.; 37 review questions.

- **39. Proofreading By Arnold Levitas**

The technical phases of the proofreader's work; reading, marking, revising, etc.; methods of handling proofs and copy. Illustrated by examples. 59 pp.; 69 review questions; glossary.

- **40. Preparation of Printers' Copy By F. W. Hamilton**

Suggestions for authors, editors, and all who are engaged in preparing copy for the composing room. 36 pp.; 67 review questions.

- **41. Printers' Manual of Style**

A reference compilation of approved rules, usages, and suggestions relating to uniformity in punctuation, capitalization, abbreviations, numerals, and kindred features of composition.

• 42. The Printer's Dictionary By A. A. Stewart

A handbook of definitions and miscellaneous information about various processes of printing, alphabetically arranged. Technical terms explained. Illustrated.

PART VII — *Design, Color, and Lettering*

• 43. Applied Design for Printers By Harry L. Gage

A handbook of the principles of arrangement, with brief comment on the periods of design which have most influenced printing. Treats of harmony, balance, proportion, and rhythm; motion; symmetry and variety; ornament, esthetic and symbolic. 37 illustrations; 46 review questions; glossary; bibliography.

• 44. Elements of Typographic Design By Harry L. Gage

Applications of the principles of decorative design. Building material of typography paper, types, ink, decorations and illustrations. Handling of shapes. Design of complete book, treating each part. Design of commercial forms and single units. Illustrations; review questions; glossary; bibliography.

[vi]

• 45. Rudiments of Color in Printing By Harry L. Gage

Use of color: for decoration of black and white, for broad poster effect, in combinations of two, three, or more printings with process engravings. Scientific nature of color, physical and chemical. Terms in which color may be discussed: hue, value, intensity. Diagrams in color, scales and combinations. Color theory of process engraving. Experiments with color. Illustrations in full color, and on various papers. Review questions; glossary; bibliography.

• 46. Lettering in Typography **By Harry L. Gage**

Printer's use of lettering: adaptability and decorative effect. Development of historic writing and lettering and its influence on type design. Classification of general forms in lettering. Application of design to lettering. Drawing for reproduction. Fully illustrated; review questions; glossary; bibliography.

• 47. Typographic Design in Advertising **By Harry L. Gage**

The printer's function in advertising. Precepts upon which advertising is based. Printer's analysis of his copy. Emphasis, legibility, attention, color. Method of studying advertising typography. Illustrations; review questions; glossary; bibliography.

• 48. Making Dummies and Layouts **By Harry L. Gage**

A layout: the architectural plan. A dummy: the imitation of a proposed final effect. Use of dummy in sales work. Use of layout. Function of layout man. Binding schemes for dummies. Dummy envelopes. Illustrations; review questions; glossary; bibliography.

PART VIII — *History of Printing*

• 49. Books Before Typography **By F. W. Hamilton**

A primer of information about the invention of the alphabet and the history of bookmaking up to the invention of movable types. 62 pp.; illustrated; 64 review questions.

- **50. The Invention of Typography By F. W. Hamilton**

A brief sketch of the invention of printing and how it came about. 64 pp.; 62 review questions.

- **51. History of Printing—Part I By F. W. Hamilton**

A primer of information about the beginnings of printing, the development of the book, the development of printers' materials, and the work of the great pioneers. 63 pp.; 55 review questions.

- **52. History of Printing—Part II By F. W. Hamilton**

A brief sketch of the economic conditions of the printing industry from 1450 to 1789, including government regulations, censorship, internal conditions and industrial relations. 94 pp.; 128 review questions.

- **53. Printing in England By F. W. Hamilton**

A short history of printing in England from Caxton to the present time. 89 pp.; 65 review questions.

- **54. Printing in America By F. W. Hamilton**

A brief sketch of the development of the newspaper, and some notes on publishers who have especially contributed to printing. 98 pp.; 84 review questions.

- **55. Type and Presses in America By F. W. Hamilton**

A brief historical sketch of the development of type casting and press building in the United States. 52 pp.; 61 review questions.

- **56. Elements of Cost in Printing By Henry P. Porter**

The Standard Cost-Finding Forms and their uses. What they should show. How to utilize the information they give. Review questions. Glossary.

• 57. Use of a Cost System **By Henry P. Porter**

The Standard Cost-Finding Forms and their uses. What they should show. How to utilize the information they give. Review questions. Glossary.

• 58. The Printer as a Merchant **By Henry P. Porter**

The selection and purchase of materials and supplies for printing. The relation of the cost of raw material and the selling price of the finished product. Review questions. Glossary.

• 59. Fundamental Principles of Estimating **By Henry P. Porter**

The estimator and his work; forms to use; general rules for estimating. Review questions. Glossary.

• 60. Estimating and Selling **By Henry P. Porter**

An insight into the methods used in making estimates, and their relation to selling. Review questions. Glossary.

• 61. Accounting for Printers **By Henry P. Porter**

A brief outline of an accounting system for printers; necessary books and accessory records. Review questions. Glossary.

PART X — *Miscellaneous*

• 62. Health, Sanitation, and Safety **By Henry P. Porter**

Hygiene in the printing trade; a study of conditions old and new; practical suggestions for improvement; protective appliances and rules for safety.

- ### 63. Topical Index By F. W. Hamilton

A book of reference covering the topics treated in the Typographic Technical Series, alphabetically arranged.

- ### 64. Courses of Study By F. W. Hamilton

A guidebook for teachers, with outlines and suggestions for classroom and shop work.

ACKNOWLEDGMENT

This series of Typographic Text-books is the result of the splendid co-operation of a large number of firms and individuals engaged in the printing business and its allied industries in the United States of America.

The Committee on Education of the United Typothetae of America, under whose auspices the books have been prepared and published, acknowledges its indebtedness for the generous assistance rendered by the many authors, printers, and others identified with this work.

While due acknowledgment is made on the title and copyright pages of those contributing to each book, the Committee nevertheless felt that a group list of co-operating firms would be of interest.

The following list is not complete, as it includes only those who have co-operated in the production of a portion of the volumes, constituting the first printing. As soon as the entire list of books comprising the Typographic Technical Series has been completed (which the Committee hopes will be at an early date), the full list will be printed in each volume.

The Committee also desires to acknowledge its indebtedness to the many subscribers to this Series who have patiently awaited its publication.

Committee on Education,
United Typothetae of America.
Henry P. Porter, *Chairman*,
E. Lawrence Fell,
A. M. Glossbrenner,
J. Clyde Oswald,
Toby Rubovits.

Frederick W. Hamilton, *Education Director*.

[ix]

CONTRIBUTORS

For Composition and Electrotypes

Isaac H. Blanchard Company, New York, N. Y.
S. H. Burbank & Co., Philadelphia, Pa.
J. S. Cushing & Co., Norwood, Mass.
The DeVinne Press, New York, N. Y.
R. R. Donnelley & Sons Co., Chicago, Ill.
Geo. H. Ellis Co., Boston, Mass.
Evans-Winter-Hebb, Detroit, Mich.
Franklin Printing Company, Philadelphia, Pa.
F. H. Gilson Company, Boston, Mass.
Stephen Greene & Co., Philadelphia, Pa.
W. F. Hall Printing Co., Chicago, Ill.
J. B. Lippincott Co., Philadelphia, Pa.
McCalla & Co. Inc., Philadelphia, Pa.
The Patteson Press, New York, New York
The Plimpton Press, Norwood, Mass.
Poole Bros., Chicago, Ill.
Edward Stern & Co., Philadelphia, Pa.
The Stone Printing & Mfg. Co., Roanoke, Va.
C. D. Traphagen, Lincoln, Neb.
The University Press, Cambridge, Mass.

For Composition

Boston Typothetae School of Printing, Boston, Mass.
William F. Fell Co., Philadelphia, Pa.
The Kalkhoff Company, New York, N. Y.
Oxford-Print, Boston, Mass.
Toby Rubovits, Chicago, Ill.

For Electrotypes

Blomgren Brothers Co., Chicago, Ill.
Flower Steel Electrotyping Co., New York, N. Y.
C. J. Peters & Son Co., Boston, Mass.
Royal Electrotype Co., Philadelphia, Pa.

H. C. Whitcomb & Co., Boston, Mass.

For Engravings

American Type Founders Co., Boston, Mass.
C. B. Cottrell & Sons Co., Westerly, R. I.
Golding Manufacturing Co., Franklin, Mass.
Harvard University, Cambridge, Mass.
Inland Printer Co., Chicago, Ill.
Lanston Monotype Machine Company, Philadelphia, Pa.
Mergenthaler Linotype Company, New York, N. Y.
Geo. H. Morrill Co., Norwood, Mass.
Oswald Publishing Co., New York, N. Y.
The Printing Art, Cambridge, Mass.
B. D. Rising Paper Company, Housatonic, Mass.
The Vandercook Press, Chicago, Ill.

For Book Paper

American Writing Paper Co., Holyoke, Mass.
West Virginia Pulp & Paper Co., Mechanicville, N. Y.